Satan:
A Biography of the Judeo Christian Prince of Darkness
By Jonathan Howard

Golgotha Press
www.golgothapress.com
© 2010

Table of Contents:

- INTRODUCTION 4
- MORNING STAR—AN ORIGIN OF GLORY 6
- THE FALL—EDEN AND THE GENESIS GAP 8
- OTHER EARLY REFERENCES—HOW MANY SATANS WERE THERE? 10
- SATAN AND THE OLD TESTAMENT 13
- SATAN OF THE NEW TESTAMENT—THE WICKED ONE 19
- COMMENTARY WORTH CONSIDERING 26
- FROM DANTE TO HOLLYWOOD—OTHER INFLUENCES 31
- MODERN VIEWS OF SATAN ACROSS RELIGIONS 34
- CONCLUSION 37

"How you have fallen from heaven, O morning star, son of the dawn! You have been cast down to earth..."
Isaiah 14

Introduction

He is called by many names in both the Old and New Testaments, as well as throughout both Judeo and Christian traditions. He is sometimes seen as a snake, a dragon, an angel of light, a terrible demon, or a single sinful thought.

Who is the one called Satan or Devil, and what do the scriptures and other ancient texts tell us about him? What have great religious thinkers and theologians written about him and his armies of demonic followers? What beliefs with reference to the devil have survived in major religions today? What influence has Satan had on Literature and popular culture throughout man's history? These are a few questions we will try to answer in the words that follow.

It might be good to start with a general overview of major beliefs people hold about the identity of Satan. There are two major ideas that we can see in scripture, in historical writings, and in churches today.

1. First, there is the classical idea of the terrible horned demon, the source of all evil. He began as a good and righteous angel, and he fell to a life of sin and wickedness.
2. The second reappearing idea about Satan claims he isn't even a person at all, but a kind of personification of sin and evil in the hearts of men.

Fallen angel or sinful desire—whatever Satan's true identity, it is undeniable that he has greatly influenced Jewish and Christian beliefs. In one-way or another, he has left his mark on human society and history, as we're about to see.

But let's start at the beginning. Where did the devil come from? Who or what was he before he was the evil angel called Satan? Let's see how these two major ideas mentioned above play out in the origin of the Wicked One.

Morning Star—an Origin of Glory

The name most commonly given to the pre-devil Satan is Lucifer. Where did that name come from? While it is based on the Bible, tradition has certainly helped it to stick.

Part of Isaiah chapter 14, quoted at the outset of this article, calls the devil "morning star". Through tradition, this title was made into a name, Lucifer, which means "light barer". In other words, at some point scribes stopped *translating* the Hebrew and starting *transliterating* it into a proper name. Although that name, Lucifer, is not mentioned anywhere else in scripture, and there is no evidence that Isaiah was giving the devil a name, Lucifer stuck, and many refer to the "pre-fall" Satan by that name.

Who or what was Lucifer? This is where the explanation divides according to our two major concepts. Let's take them one at a time.

The most ancient of traditions puts Lucifer as a faithful and good angel created by god. He may have been the head of many other angels, or an archangel. According to this concept, Lucifer was in a privileged position before God, and at some point he was put in charge of the Garden of Eden. That goodness, however, was only skin deep, which was made evident when he "fell" into sin and rebellion.

As for the second concept, seeing Satan as the sinful inclination in the hearts of man means that he wouldn't be around until man was created. He would, in effect be *born* when Eve first saw and desired the forbidden fruit in Genesis. We'll return to this view later, when we examine more carefully the account in Eden. But first, let's look at some pre-biblical and extra-biblical ideas regarding the origin of the devil. To start with, we'll examine just how a good and pure angel would have become the agent of evil and darkness.

The Fall—Eden and the Genesis Gap

How do we get from the glorious angel Lucifer, who was possibly an archangel or cherub, to the nasty and evil creature of modern tradition? The most popular story takes place in the Garden of Eden.

Lucifer was already a powerful angel, but he wanted more power and glory for himself. He wanted to be worshiped like a god. When God created man and woman, the temptation was simply too much for Lucifer. Either transforming himself into a snake, or using a snake as a puppet, he convinced Eve to eat of the forbidden fruit. Eve, in turn, convinced Adam, and sin was born on the earth.

After this, Lucifer is still seen ascending and descending to and from heaven, and it's curious that the judgments from God were pronounced against Adam, Eve, and the serpent, but not Lucifer. But from this point on, he is called Satan and is always seen in a bad or negative light. The fall continues as the devil seems to grow more and more wicked through history, until at some point he is actually cast out from heaven by Michael, another archangel.

There is, however, another tradition regarding Satan's fall, one that predates Adam himself. This has to do with what is called the "Genesis Gap Doctrine". What is that exactly?

Many believe that there was a flood, like that of Noah's day, before Adam. This explains why fossils of dinosaurs are found today while they're not mentioned in the bible. The idea comes from a possible gap between the first two verses of Genesis, where it first says that God created the heavens and the earth, and then it describes the earth as being filled with water and being "void" or in ruin.

What kind of world was there before it was covered with water in verse two? It's impossible to know. But the "Genesis Gap Doctrine" does explain why scientists say our planet is much older than the traditional 6,000 years. Could both be right? With the Genesis Gap it seems possible. Now, how does Lucifer/Satan come into all of this?

This pre-Adam world may have been destroyed due to the wrong actions of Lucifer and his angelic followers. That means, Satan's true fall may have been long before Eden and the forbidden fruit. But, because there are no writings or records of this hypothetical pre-Adam world, we cannot say how or why Lucifer rebelled in this ancient Earth before Eden and Adam.

Other Early References— How Many Satans Were There?

Aside from the mysterious Genesis Gap, there are other pre-Christian, extra-biblical references to Satan, specifically Jewish tradition and the so-called apocryphal writings. What do we learn about Satan from these?

In Rabbinic Literature, we find two major ideas about the creation or origin or Satan. The most common and supported is the same as what we've said before—that Satan is a fallen angel. The other idea states that Satan was created on the Sixth day, just like Eve. Satan also exists in Rabbinic tradition and texts as the evil impulse of man, or his sinful desires. In this form, he is called Yetzer ha Ra. The Talmud gives strength to both the external person of Satan, as well as this Yetzer ha Ra present in the minds and hearts of every man.

In many older texts, there are in fact many Satans, like a whole league of them headed by a big Boss Satan. This sounds very similar to the devil and his demons of later Christian teachings. A great example of this is in 1 Enoch. While the Talmud allows for the two Satans mentioned above, the external and internal, 1 Enoch talks about up to 5 different Satans. Two of them convinced some of God's angels to rebel and come down to Earth, having their way with the daughters of mankind and procreating giants. A third and separate Satan is said to be responsible for Adam and Eve's folly and rebellion. Another Satan gives man the ability to read and write!

Eventually, Jewish traditional texts start to combine these multiple visions of Satan into one epitome of Evil. He is then seen as the single leader of the fallen angels, or demons. At some point, Yetzer ha Ra (mentioned above as wickedness in the hearts of man) and the external Satan are seen as the same person. So, through Rabbinic history, we go from two Satans, to many, and then to one.

Over time, this new, unified Satan is given greater and greater power. Not only is he counted as the active agent in mankind's fall, but as the source of all evil. Rabbis begin to blame Satan for every tragedy and mistake in Jewish history. Satan is stipulated as the true father of Cain (a forerunner of the Incubus?), because only the Father of Evil could inspire the first ever murderer. Satan is also made responsible for any tragedy that befalls the Jewish people or their ancestors. The devil is even blamed for the almost-sacrifice of Abraham's son, Isaac! (Genesis chapter 22)

Thus far, we've seen quite a lot of back-history and tradition referring to the devil. But the most well-known source of information about Satan, or any other Judeo-Christian personage, for that matter, is of course the Bible itself. Where is Satan mentioned in both the Old and New Testament? What can we learn about him through scripture? That's what we'll see next.

Satan and the Old Testament

There are two major mentions of Satan in the Old Testament—the serpent in the Garden of Eden, and the accuser in the book of Job. We'll look first at Job for two reasons. First, Job is one of the older, if not the oldest, books in the Old Testament, and second, it takes priority because Satan is specifically named, whereas in Genesis he isn't.

In the account of Job, Satan enters the "throne room" of God, and God asks him where he's been. Satan answers that he's been walking about on the earth, and it comes to light that he's been taking special note of God's servant, Job. Satan claims that Job only serves God because He protects and blesses him. God allows the devil to test Job.

Satan, with God's permission, takes away everything that Job has—his family, his house, his livestock and servants. He's left with nothing, but he still keeps his integrity. Satan then challenges Job before God again, saying that a man would give anything to keep his own life. God allows Satan to take things a bit further. Job is struck with disease, and left to scratch at his painful boils with broken pieces of pottery. Then, supposed comforters come and begin to accuse Job of being a bad person. Through all of this, Job keeps his integrity. Afterward, God rewards Job for his faithfulness.

There are several interesting features of this story that reveal something about Satan. First, the devil could not do anything without God's permission. He also could travel freely between Heaven and Earth. He isn't seen as evil, but more devious, as an accuser or prosecutor.

It's also interesting that Job himself did not think that a devil or demon was doing something to him. He believed God himself was causing his suffering, as if he didn't even know who Satan was! The devil's actions in this story are interestingly indirect. He never attacked Job directly, nor did he reveal himself to anyone. Instead, he acted as an impersonal force, through robbers and barbarians and natural forces and disease.

Reading the book of Job, one may not see Satan as a wicked spirit at all, but a member of God's heavenly court, whose job it is to test His physical creation, just as he did to Job. This idea of this is still common today, as we'll see later on.

The other major mention of Satan, though not as a direct mention of any kind, is in Genesis, in the Garden of Eden. The serpent that tempted Eve is never identified as the devil in the Old Testament, but in Revelation, Satan is called the "original serpent", referring back to the story of Eden. What do we see of the devil in this account?

Here Satan transforms into a snake to talk to Eve, or else uses a serpent as a puppet. In catholic tradition, he actually used a small dragon to speak to Eve, and later when God pronounced judgment on the sinners, he plucked the wings and legs from the dragon, turning it into the first ever snake. Generally, however, it is believed that Satan used an ordinary serpent, hanging conveniently from a tree nearby Eve. The serpent first asked Eve if it's really the case that they could not eat of the forbidden fruit, from the tree of the knowledge of good and evil. Eve answered truthfully. Then the snake pronounced what many believe to be the first lie in the history of the universe, saying that Eve certainly would not die. He then proceeded to say that eating of the fruit would open her eyes and make her like God, knowing the difference between good and bad.

That snake did more than lie to Eve about the fruit. He slandered, or lied against, God, saying, in effect, that God was hiding something good from them, and that he is really a bad ruler and they should not listen to him anymore. The name "devil" by the way, means slanderer, which is fitting for this story. This is why we can say that the disobedience was a true rebellion of the part of Adam, Eve, and the Snake, or Satan. Eve, of course, followed the snake's directions and ate of the fruit, and later offered it to her husband, who also sinned by eating of it. There is quite the variety of interpretations of the Eden account and the Fall of Man, but traditionally Satan is held at least partially responsible for this fall.

The two major concepts regarding the identity of Satan presented at the beginning of this article can be easily seen in the story of the Garden of Eden:

1. The fallen Angel, once called Lucifer, becomes Satan in the act of deceiving Eve. He does this (as mentioned above) in order to gain control over the humans, since he wants to be worshiped like a god.
2. "Satan" as a personification of the evil in the hearts of men, is born when Eve looks at the forbidden fruit and reasons within herself that God is keeping something good from her. She takes the fruit and offers it to here husband. Evil is born into the world, and the devil is given life as the perfect scapegoat for every sin and mistake ("The devil made me do it.").

Whichever interpretation you may choose to follow, the fact remains that the serpent is never given the name Satan in the entire account, leading many historians to believe that it wasn't the devil at all. Aside from these two major stories in the Old Testament that involve Satan, there are two other texts of interest. Let's look at those now. The first we have already seen, partially quoted at the outset of this article. Let's see what Isaiah chapter 14 tells us about Satan.

The expressions "morning star" or "shining star" (depending on the translation) give us the name Lucifer for the angel that later rebelled and became Satan. From this verse, we also see pride as a reason for his fall. "For you said to yourself, `I will ascend to heaven and set my throne above God's stars. I will preside on the mountain of the gods far away in the north.'"

Satan apparently wanted what he did not have, and he was willing to break God's laws to receive worship from others. He has long been used to teach a lesson in the dangers of pride. Did Lucifer get what he wanted? Isaiah answers, "But instead, you will be brought down to the place of the dead, down to its lowest depths."

Ezekiel also has something to tell us about the devil, before we leave the Old Testament for the New. In chapter 38, he is described as having been in the Garden of Eden. "You were in Eden, the garden of God. Your clothing was adorned with every precious stone—red carnelian, chrysolite, white moonstone, beryl, onyx, jasper, sapphire, turquoise, and emerald—all beautifully crafted for you and set in the finest gold. They were given to you on the day you were created."

The pre-fall Satan is here described as a beautiful and precious angel, covered in figurative stones of great value. Placing him in Eden, Ezekiel also backs up the suggestion that Satan was responsible for the talking serpent in Genesis.

Ezekiel continues, "I ordained and anointed you as the mighty angelic guardian. You had access to the holy mountain of God and walked among the stones of fire." This quote also complies with what is written in Job, how Satan could come and go between Heaven and Earth as he pleased. This also shows that Satan had some kind of great privilege as Lucifer the angel, perhaps even as an Archangel, as some theologians claim.

Ezekiel also explains that Satan was full or pride, and was punished by being banished to the earth, unable to ascend to heaven any longer, saying, "So I banished you from the mountain of God. I expelled you…I threw you to the earth and exposed you to the curious gaze of kings."

These four major references to the devil in the Old Testament, in Genesis, Job, Ezekiel and Isaiah, show us a fallen angel, a tempter, and a accuser. We also see at least some evidence for the concept of Satan being an aspect of human sinfulness. But what about the horrible monster many think of regarding Satan? What about the great dragon, or the wild beast? In the New Testament, Satan takes on a new form, as we'll see in the next section.

Satan of the New Testament—The Wicked One

Through the centuries, Satan has morphed and evolved from a beautiful angel and accuser, to a rough and ugly monster. The bulk of this change can be easily spotted in the New Testament. In the references that follow, we'll also see plenty of evidence to support our two major concepts regarding the identity of Satan, as well as a continuation of some of the themes we've seen thus far.

The first and most extensive account in which Satan appears is in Matthew chapter 4, where he tempts Jesus. Let's look at this story more carefully, because there is a lot to learn here. The account starts with a hungry Jesus, since he has just spent 40 days in the wilderness alone, without any food. It is in this state that Satan visits him, to tempt him. What we see that follows is a series of three temptations from the devil to Jesus. Each of these shows us something about how Satan was viewed at the time, and would be viewed after.

The first temptation goes like this, "Then the Devil came and said to him, 'If you are the Son of God, change these stones into loaves of bread.'" Here Satan is tempting Jesus by taking advantage of his hungry condition, and he is therefore seen as an opportunist. We'll see this same theme played out later in the New Testament.

The second temptation is very interesting, since it can be seen more as a dare. "Then the Devil took him to Jerusalem, to the highest point of the Temple, and said, 'If you are the Son of God, jump off! For the Scriptures say, "He orders his angels to protect you. And they will hold you with their hands to keep you from striking your foot on a stone."'" This dare-making, accusing, taunting devil reminds us of the Satan of Job. We also see that Satan must be aware of what is written in scripture, because he quotes from the bible itself.

The third and final temptation reveals something very interesting about the Satan of the New Testament. "Next the Devil took him to the peak of a very high mountain and showed him the nations of the world and all their glory. 'I will give it all to you,' he said, 'if you will only kneel down and worship me.'" Why is this final test, or temptation, interesting? First, we see the old concept of Satanic pride, always wanting worship that does not belong to him. But we also learn something about the power that the devil has in Matthew. He apparently owns the governments of the world.

This is a recurring theme of the Greek Scriptures. Satan is shown as the ruler and owner of the world and it's political institutions. How else could he offer such to Jesus in Matthew chapter 4? And if Satan did not really have authority to give such glory to Jesus, would it really have been a "temptation" to him? According to Matthew, Satan is the owner of the world.

This idea is brought up again in the New Testament, this time in John, in his first letter (1 John 5:19). He says that the whole world is lying in the power of the wicked one. What an interesting change! In Job, Satan could not even change the life of one man without God's permission, and now he has complete control over the whole world.

Shifting from submissive member of God's heavenly court to ruler of the world is not the only change Satan undergoes in the Gospels. In John chapter 8, Satan is described as a murderer and father of the lie. What does that mean? The devil might well be called the father or originator of the lie because of the first lie the serpent told Eve in Eden, that she would not die as a result of eating of the forbidden fruit.

Why, though, is Satan called a manslayer, or murderer? It may also be a reference to Genesis, because in 1 John, Cain (who murdered his brother, Abel) is said to have originated with the wicked one. This fits, because Jesus said of the devil in John 8:44, "That one was a manslayer when he began." This may remind us of the Jewish tradition, mentioned earlier, that Satan was the real father of Cain.

Satan's image continues to worsen through the Greek Scriptures. Peter wrote in his first letter (1 Peter 5:18), "Be careful! Watch out for attacks from the Devil, your great enemy. He prowls around like a roaring lion, looking for some victim to devour." Here, Satan is called "your enemy". Not God's enemy, yours. He's also likened to a great a ferocious beast—a lion.

This is a subtle but important change in imagery. Until now, he was seen more as a slippery, sneaky, tempting, lying snake. He was more mischievous than evil. But now, as a lion on the prowl, he's searching for someone to devour. The idea of Satan being every good Christian's enemy is taken even further by John, Paul, and James, as we'll se next.

As we already saw, John wrote that the entire world was lying in the power, or hand, of the wicked one, Satan. The very fact that Satan was called a wicked one is noteworthy, but not isolated to this one verse. John also writes of ones that have conquered the wicked one. (1 John 2)

Paul, likewise says in his letter to the Ephesians that we must wear a kind of spiritual armor, including "faith as your shield to stop the fiery arrows aimed at you by Satan," (Ephesians 6:16) or the wicked one. This provokes a powerful image of a literal spiritual battle, in which good people are being attacked by the devil himself.

James likewise writes in Chapter 4 of his book, "So humble yourselves before God. Resist the Devil, and he will flee from you. Draw close to God, and God will draw close to you." Satan is again shown as an evil force in direct conflict with God and His will. A spiritual man would have to resist, or fight against the attacks and trickery of Satan to stay close to God.

Yes, the Devil is brought out from the sidelines and background in the New Testament, he places himself in the front line, along with his armies of demons. To quote again from Paul's writing in Ephesians 6:11,

"Put on all of God's armor so that you will be able to stand firm against *all strategies and tricks of the Devil*. For we are not fighting against people made of flesh and blood, but against the evil rulers and authorities of the unseen world, against *those mighty powers of darkness* who rule this world, and against wicked spirits in the heavenly realms. Use every piece of God's armor to resist the enemy in the time of evil, so that after the battle you will still be standing firm." (Italics not in original Bible text)

The most evil and dastardly representation of Satan, however, is seen in Revelation. We saved this for last because it reminds us most of the horned and savage looking Satan of more modern mythology. In revelation, Satan is characterized by a Great Dragon.

Before we see what the bible says of Satan in Revelation, it may be best to remember what exactly a dragon is. Movies of knights and ladies and dragons may be fun to watch, but in ancient time a dragon was more like a large snake. Similar to the Chinese dragon, the Greek word originally used forms the idea of a great devouring snake. Interestingly, this idea was passed along from Greek to Latin, and even to Romance languages like Spanish. In Spanish to swallow or devour is to *tragar*. A shot, as in shot of whiskey, is a *trago*. Someone who eats a lot or food, devouring it we can say, may be called *tragon*, which looks and sounds a lot like dragon.

So when we see Revelation calling Satan a dragon, we should imagine a large and hungry snake, and not the fire-breathing dinosaur in popular movies and games.

What, then does the book of Revelation say about this Dragon, or Satan? We can see in Revelation chapter 12. The chapter opens with a celestial woman giving birth to a son, as she struggles in her birth pangs, Satan shows up. Notice how he's described:

> "Suddenly, I witnessed in heaven another significant event. I saw a large red dragon with seven heads and ten horns, with seven crowns on his heads. His tail dragged down one-third of the stars, which he threw to the earth. He stood before the woman as she was about to give birth to her child, ready to devour the baby as soon as it was born."

Here the devil is ready to kill this small child. When the baby is born, however, God saves it and hides the woman out in the desert. What happens now to the dragon?

Michael the Archangle battles the dragon and its "demons" or "angels". Satan loses, and is thrown out of heaven down to the Earth. That's why we see this warning: "But terror will come on the earth and the sea. For the Devil has come down to you in great anger, and he knows that he has little time."

At the conclusion of the chapter, the dragon wages war with the other children of the woman, and anyone claiming to be with Jesus. The next chapter continues with this dragon, and now a great and mighty beast worships it, because Satan had given it its power.

Here we also find the mysterious number, or "mark", of the beast, 666. Interestingly, it's a little known fact that this number 666 doesn't belong to the devil, but to the beast. The bible says it's "a man's number" or "the number of mankind."

Later in Revelation, we find the end of the Devil. He is first thrown into an abyss for a thousand years, and then he's let loose for a short while in order to test mankind one last time. Then he is destroyed, or thrown into a lake of fire, forever. And thus is the foretold end of Satan in the bible.

As you can see, Satan changed greatly through the scriptures, from a simple angel, to a great and powerful dragon and ruler of all evil. Does the study of Satan stop with Revelation? Not at all! In the subheading that follows, we'll look into even more of Satan's legendary existence.

Commentary Worth Considering

Satan's story doesn't end with the completion of the bible. In the last 20 centuries or so since the New Testament was written, Christianity has grown from a small and illegal sect to the official religion of the Roman empire, to a variety of world religions. Throughout this time numerous theologians and religious writers have recorded further thoughts and conclusions regarding the devil. We'll see a few of these now.

The first of these scholars that we'll look at is Saint Augustine, or Augustine of Hippo. He lived in the 4th Century AD, and his views of Satan change very little with what we read in scripture, although it seems that the common view of the people had started to change, and in his writings he tried to pull them back, as it were.

At this time, persecution again Christianity had virtually stopped. The Jewish system had—for all intents and purposes—ended in 70 AD with the fall of Rome, and the Roman Empire itself no longer hunted Christians, since Christianity was the official religion of Rome after the conversion of Constantine. How did this affect people's view of the devil? Well, in the first couple of centuries after Christ, any opposition or persecution Christians faced was seen as an attack by Satan. When these trials started to disappear, so did Satan's presence in daily religious conversation.

Augustine saw Satan as real and still powerful. He saw mankind in sin and therefore under the influence of the devil. He wrote in Marriage and Concupiscence: "The human race is the Devil's fruit tree, his own property, from which he may pick his fruit. It is a plaything of demons."

While he was keenly aware and freely broadcasting the existence of Satan, Augustine could never come to terms with his origin. He believed that God created all things, and that all that God creates is good, therefore evil can't possibly exist. He viewed that Satan must have been good in the beginning, but elsewhere he postulated that he was born evil. What messy condradictions! But these examples are good for us to look into because they foreshadow the confusion that still thrives in modern churches, as we'll soon see.

Let's bring ourselves forward, to Thomas Aquinas of the 13th century. What did he say about the origin of Satan? Had this problem been worked out? In a word, yes. Aquinas had worked out an extensive explanation behind Satan's origin and pre-fall nature. Much of this concept is still held by the Catholic Church.

Aquinas believed that Satan was originally an Angel, and that he had fallen due to pride. These are themes, of course, that you'll recognize from above. Satan was created a good and holy angel, but he then chose to sin. Therefore God did not create evil, but evil is the fall—or corrupted—of the good of God. Satan sinfully tried to increase his own glory, to make himself greater than God, and in this sin of pride, he convinced other angels to follow him into ruin.

It's interesting that Aquinas did not think Satan was an Archangel, as previously discussed. Instead, he had a complete organization of angels, separated into three separate orders. Archangels, according to Aquinas, belong, not at the top as leaders of other angels, but at the bottom. They are the executers and physical workers, doing the will of God.

Aquinas wrote that Satan must have been a Cherub. The Cherubim belonged to the highest order, and they are the ones usually depicted as little babies in heaven. They are characterized by their innocence, power, and knowledge. Satan was seen by Aquinas as both powerful and knowledgeable, and he proposed that Satan lost his innocence when he fell into sin.

Satan and his demonic angels, all called devils by Aquinas, have permanently fallen into sin, and cannot be redeemed. By the same token, those angelic servants that stayed faithful are now incapable of sin, because they've proven themselves good and holy forever. In this way, Aquinas easily explained the duality of good and evil, as well as sin and evil's origin.

We see, though, that not all biblical scholars of history taught the same ideas. Martin Luther, who lived in the 15th and 16th centuries, believed that Satan was created as Lucifer, the greatest of the angels. He was jealous of God's partiality for humans, choosing to take a man's form and not an angel's. Lucifer rebelled and was thrown down to the earth, where he became Satan, the archenemy of God and ruler over mankind.

Luther taught that God and the devil were fighting over human souls, but he often said that we as humans have no say in the matter. He likened us to horses who cannot control our riders.

Luther also saw suffering and difficulties in life to be from both the devil and God, as if they were working together. He believed that Satan and God might bring about the same evil in one's life, but for different purposes. Even today, many Lutherans cannot fully understand his thoughts on these matters. Scholars say that even Luther himself was likely unclear as to who was behind some of the suffering in his life.

Nonetheless, Luther was known as an opposer of the devil. One quite commonly attributed to him says, "I often laugh at Satan, and there is nothing that makes him so angry as when I attack him to his face, and tell him that through God I am more than a match for him." There is even a story—some say myth, some say fact—about Luther throwing an inkwell at the devil, when Satan was trying to deceive him by appearing as Christ.

Another interesting reformer is John Calvin, also from the 16th century. He minimalized Satan, almost out of existence. Some biblical texts commonly applied to Satan, like Isaiah chapter 14, quoted above, had nothing to do with the devil in Calvin's mind.

Calvin did recognize that Satan existed. He wrote in *Institutes of the Christian Religion*, "Remember that Satan has miracles, too." But he did not blame Satan for mankind's fall. He believed that evil came from the hearts of man, and did not have to exist outside of it.

Talking about this same time period, *The New Encyclopædia Britannica* states: "In the aftermath of the 16th-century Copernican revolution (based on the theories of the Polish astronomer Copernicus), in which the Earth was no longer seen as the centre of the cosmos but, instead, merely as a planet of a solar system that is a very small part of a galaxy in an apparently infinite universe—the concepts of angels and demons no longer seemed appropriate."

As you can see, Luther's and Calvin's views were very different from those of previous Catholic scholars. In fact, we can still see this division in opinion in modern churches, as we'll consider in a later subheading. But first, let's take a moment to look at Satan as portrayed in literature and eventually film.

From Dante to Hollywood—Other Influences

You may or may not see literature and film as a reliable source of information. But the fact is, great writers like Dante and Milton changed the way people thought about God, Angels, Hell, and the devil himself. Today, all that most people know about Satan is what they see of him on the big screen. We cannot bring ourselves forward to the modern beliefs regarding Satan without first considering this source of influence.
Dante wrote his Divine Comedy sometime in the final years of his life, in the early 14th century. His first installment, or part, Inferno deals with one man's travels to the depths of hell to rescue his love. In the final, lowest, darkest part of hell lives the fallen angel Lucifer, or Satan. He's described as a great and demonic creature with three mouths and huge powerful wings. His dragon-like wings caused winds to blow out to the other parts of hell. In his three mouths were three legendary sinners, Judas, Brutus, and Cassius.

What's interesting about Satan in Dante's work isn't that he's a huge monster. That was seen since the writing of Revelation. Dante saw Satan, not as the ruler of all evil, but as a fellow prisoner in hell. Satan was entrapped by ice and unable to escape. He was just as much a victim as any other sinner in the inferno. This view deeply affected people's views, all the way from the renaissance to now.

Another classical piece of literature that discussed Satan in great detail is John Milton's Paradise Lost. Here, much of the story is seen through the eyes of Lucifer as he falls and becomes the devil. Milton portrays angelic minds as more refined human minds, with human thoughts. In Milton's work, we see the devil's decision to fall in an interesting new light:

> "So farwel Hope, and with Hope farwel Fear,
> Farwel Remorse: all Good to me is lost;
> Evil be thou my Good;"

With those words, Satan gave up the good and embraced the evil and wicked, as if it were a logical and almost natural choice. At the same time, he speaks as if he's dooming himself, and therefore sounds almost regretful of his own fall.

As we come forward in time, to the silver screen, we see the devil portrayed, not in simple illustrations and paintings, but by flesh and blood actors and computer generated imaging. In the last two decades alone the number of demon-related movies and television series is astronomical. From the famous book and movie The Exorcist, to movies like End of Days, and The Rite, we see people seeking to be entertained by wild and savage portrayals of demons, demonic possessions, and Satan himself.

These movies certainly have had a great impact on how the general population views Satan. As we'll see in the next subheading, major religious views greatly differ regarding who Satan is, and the teachers and theologians within church orders can't even always agree. Let's look at a summary of what we've seen throughout this article, indeed, throughout the centuries, and let's boil it down to what is believed and taught in various Christian faiths.

Modern Views of Satan across Religions

Today, the same basic beliefs in Satan exist. We can see our two main ideas regarding the devil show up in every major Christian religion. Let's look at them again, one at a time, and focus on some of the little differences:

Satan As a Real Person and Fallen Angel

The first major concept regarding Satan's existence involves the idea that he is a fallen angel. As we've seen, there are some differences in the details. For example, did Satan fall before or after the rebellion in Eden? Was his name really Lucifer before his fall? Was he really responsible for Adam's sin?

The Catholics, for example, will say that he was a Cherub, and he did fall, and that he is responsible, at least if part, for the sin in Eden. Among Orthodox and Protestant churches, Lucifer may or may not be used, and man may take more heat for Eden's rebellion. Others of Protestant faiths may say that Satan was an Archangel, and that Archangels are the leaders of all the other angels.

Another side belief, seen as far back as ancient rabbinic texts, shows that Satan is not truly evil, but an angel working for God as a tempter or tester. According to this unpopular but nonetheless surviving view, Satan is like a prosecuting lawyer, sent by God to test his creation. Such a view fits nicely with the books of Job, Genesis, and even Mathew. There are many Protestant churches that still hold this teaching.

Also, among all Christian faiths, belief in the devil as a real person has been pasted over with scientific discovery. Our view of the universe today leaves little room for powerful angels and demons. Even in the Catholic churches, whose official teachings confirm Satan's existence, do not put much emphasis on the fallen angel. When asked "is Satan real?" many poled clergy claimed to believe in him, but had trouble "personalizing him." In other words, they saw him more as a force of evil than a real person.

Satan is Just the Evil in the Hearts of Man

This second belief has taken on real shape in recent centuries. Labeling the devil as a force of evil, as the personification of bad and sin in the hearts of men makes more sense to many theologians today, especially those of Lutheran and Orthodox faiths.

Just as the clergy mentioned above, Satan is seem more and more as something difficult to personalize. Some official church teaching actual say that to believe that Satan is real and powerful is to say that we are not truly responsible for our own actions. Therefore, the devil is seen more and more as a creation of human sinfulness.

With modern science and skepticism, Satan and the demons are seen as mythological creatures, like Zeus or Hades. He's seen as the result of special effects in movies and video games. People who believe in him as a wicked spirit are made fun of, being called superstitious and naïve.

Conclusion

Will we see a return to the belief in the Dragon, the roaring lion, the master of evil that Satan once was? Will people again cower in the shadows as they walk the streets, afraid that the devil might be around the next corner? Or is that entire Mythos dead or quickly dying, and Satan is now forever reserved for the religiously fanatical? It's hard to say. In effect, we've seen, through scripture, religion, commentary, literature, and film, the rise and fall of the devil. And just as he was cast down to the earth in the bible, he has been cast down to legend and myth in so many people's minds.

With the horrendous problems we see in the world today, and so much suffering at the hands of mere humans, we no longer need a Satan to explain wickedness. Evil is almost tangible and real in itself. We need no dragon or demon or monster. We have dictators, promoters of genocide, drug lords, and pedophiles to personify evil today, and none of them need have horns on their heads to be thought of as wicked.

But one thing is certain: As long as religion is around, as long as we believe in good, and as long as we have hope, there will also be evil. And with evil, there will always be a Satan in one form or another. He will continue to test, torture, and strike fear into the hearts of mankind, whether he be found in movies, in religious books, or in a guilty conscience and our own reflection. The devil is here to stay, in one form or another, if anything, as a reflection into the darkest parts of our very own souls.

Printed in Great Britain
by Amazon